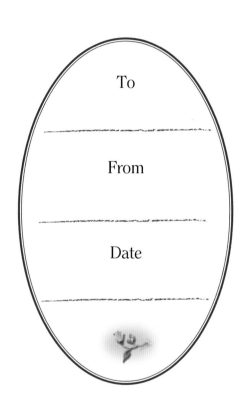

To

_____

From

_____

Date

_____

The Heart of a Mother

© 2006 Christian Art Gifts, RSA
        Christian Art Gifts Inc., IL, USA

Artwork copyright © 2006 by Cathi Freund, licensed by
Suzanne Cruise
Designed by Christian Art Gifts

Printed in China

ISBN 1-86920-357-7

06 07 08 09 10 11 12 13 14 15 – 10 9 8 7 6 5 4 3 2

The Heart of a Mother

Helen Steiner Rice™

Artwork by Cathi Freund

Contents

Mother

In all this world through all of time
there could not be another
who could fulfill God's purpose
as completely as a mother!

Mother is
a word called love

Mother is a word called love
and all the world is mindful of
the love that's given
and shown to others
is different from the love of mothers.

For mothers play the leading roles
in giving birth to little souls,
for though small souls are heaven-sent
and we realize they're only lent,
it takes a mother's loving hands
and her gentle heart that understands
to mold and shape this little life
and shelter it
through storm and strife.

So mothers are a special race
God sent to earth to take His place
and mother is a lovely name
that even saints are proud to claim.

Love is patient, love is kind.
It does not envy,
it does not boast, it is not proud.
It always protects,
always trusts, always hopes,
always perseveres.

1 CORINTHIANS 13:4, 7

Mother's advice

Sometimes when a light
goes out of our life
and we are left
in darkness
and do not know
which way to go,
we must put our hand
into the hand of God
and ask Him to lead us ...

And if we let our life
become a prayer
until we are strong enough
to stand under the weight
of our own thoughts again,
somehow even the most difficult
hours are bearable.

Flowers leave their fragrance

This old Chinese proverb,
if practiced each day,
would change the whole world
in a wonderful way -

Its truth is so simple,
it's easy to do,
and it works every time
and successfully, too -

For you can't do a kindness
without a reward,
not in silver nor gold
but in joy from the Lord -

You can't light a candle
to show others the way
without feeling the warmth
of that bright little ray -

12

And you can't pluck a rose,
all fragrant with dew,
without part of its fragrance
remaining with you.

And whose hands bestow
more fragrant bouquets
than Mother who daily
speaks kind words of praise -

A mother whose courage
and comfort and cheer
light bright little candles
in hearts through the year -

No wonder the hands
of an unselfish mother
are symbols of sweetness
unlike any other.

The priceless gift

The priceless gift of life is love,
for with the help of God above
love can change the human race
and make this world a better place.
For love dissolves all hate and fear
and makes our vision bright and clear
so we can see and rise above
our pettiness on wings of love.

Life's richest treasure

Life's richest treasure
that money cannot measure
is a mother's love,
a heart gift from God above.

Sons are a heritage
from the LORD,
children a reward from Him.
Like arrows in the hands
of a warrior are
sons born in one's youth.

PSALM 127:3-4

A prayer for patience

God, teach me to be patient,
teach me to go slow,
teach me how to wait on You
when my way I do not know.

Teach me sweet forbearance
when things do not go right
so I remain unruffled
when others grow uptight.

Teach me how to quiet
my racing, rising heart
so I may hear the answer
You are trying to impart.

Teach me to let go, dear God,
and pray undisturbed until
my heart is filled with inner peace
and I learn to know Your will!

A Mother's Day Prayer

Our Father in heaven
whose love is divine,
thanks for the love
of a mother like mine.

And in Thy great mercy
look down from above
and grant this dear mother
the gift of Your love.

And all through the year,
whatever betide her,
assure her each day
that You are beside her.

And, Father in heaven,
show me the way
to lighten her tasks
and brighten her day.

And bless her dear heart
with the insight to see
that her love means more
than the world to me.

He settles
the barren woman
in her home
as a happy mother
of children.
PSALM 113:9

On
Mother's Day

No other love
than mother love
could do the things
required of
the one to whom
God gives the keeping
of His wee lambs,
awake or sleeping.

A many-splendored miracle

A mother's love is something
that no one can explain,
it is made of deep devotion
and of sacrifice and pain.

It is endless and unselfish
and enduring come what may,
for nothing can destroy it
or take that love away.

It is patient and forgiving
when all others are forsaking,
and it never fails or falters
even though the heart is breaking.

It believes beyond believing
when the world around condemns,
and it glows with all the beauty
of the rarest, brightest gems.

It is far beyond defining,
it defies all explanation,
and it still remains a secret
like the mysteries of creation.

A many-splendored miracle
man cannot understand,
and another wondrous evidence
of God's tender guiding hand.

Motherhood

The dearest gifts that heaven holds,
the very finest, too,
were made into one pattern
that was perfect, sweet, and true;
the angels smiled, well-pleased,
and said: "Compared to all the others,
the pattern is so wonderful
let's use it just for mothers!"
And through the years, a mother
has been all that's sweet and good
for there's a bit of God and love,
in all true motherhood.

Her children *arise* and call her *blessed*;
her husband *also*,
and he *praises* her:
"Many women do *noble things*,
but you *surpass* them all."

PROVERBS 31:28-29

25

A mother's love

A mother's love is like an island
in life's ocean vast and wide,
a peaceful, quiet shelter
from the restless, rising tide.

A mother's love is like a fortress
and we seek protection there
when the waves of tribulation
seem to drown us in despair.

A mother's love is a sanctuary
where our souls can find sweet rest
from the struggle and the tension
of life's fast and futile quest.

A mother's love is like a tower
rising far above the crowd,
and her smile is like the sunshine
breaking through a threatening cloud.

A mother's love is like a beacon
burning bright with faith and prayer,
and through the changing scenes of life
we can find a haven there.

For a mother's love is fashioned
after God's enduring love,
it is endless and unfailing
like the love of Him above.

The LORD blesses
the home
of the righteous.

PROVERBS 3:33

Where there is love

Where there is love the heart is light,
Where there is love the day is bright,
Where there is love there is a song
To help when things are going wrong.
Where there is love there is a smile
to make all things seem more worthwhile,
where there is love there's quiet peace,
a tranquil place where turmoils cease -
love changes darkness into light
and makes the heart take "wingless flight".

Everyone needs
someone

Everyone needs someone
to be thankful for,
and each day of life
we are aware of this more,
for the joys of enjoying
and the fullness of living
are found in the hearts of mothers
that are filled with thanksgiving!

As a mother
comforts her child,
so will I
comfort you.
ISAIAH 66:13

Now I lay me down to sleep

I remember so well this prayer I said
each night as my mother
tucked me in bed.

And today this same prayer
is still the best way
to sign off with God
at the end of the day
and to ask Him
your soul to safely keep
as you wearily close tired eyes in sleep,
feeling content that the Father above
will hold you secure
in His great arms of love.

And having His promise
that if e'er you don't wake
His angels will reach down
your sweet soul to take
is perfect assurance
that awake or asleep
God is always right there
to tenderly keep
all of His children
ever safe in His care.

For God's here and He's there
and He's everywhere,
so into His hands each night as I sleep
I commit my soul
for the dear Lord to keep,
knowing that if my soul
should take flight
it will soar to the land
where there is no night.

Enfolded in His love

The love of God surrounds us
like the air we breathe around us -
As near as a heartbeat,
as close as a prayer,
and whenever we need Him
He'll always be there!

He tends His flock like a shepherd:
He gathers the lambs in His arms
and carries them close to His heart;
He gently leads those that have young.

ISAIAH 40:11

At my mother's knee

I have worshiped
in churches and chapels,
I have prayed in the busy street,
I have sought my God
and have found Him
where the waves of the ocean beat.

I have knelt in a silent forest,
in the shade of an ancient tree,
but the dearest of all my altars
was raised at my mother's knee.

God, make me the woman of her vision
and purge me of all selfishness,
and keep me true to her standards
and help me to live to bless
and then keep me a pilgrim forever
at the shrine of my mother's knee.

*I remember the days
of long ago;
I meditate on all Your works
and consider what Your
hands have done.*

PSALM 143:5

Memories
are a treasure

Memories are a treasure
time cannot take away,
so may you be surrounded
by happy ones today.
May all the love and tenderness
of golden years well spent
come back today to fill your heart
with beauty and content.

Deep in my heart

Happy little memories
go flitting through my mind
and in all my thoughts
and memories
I always seem to find
the picture of your face, Mother,
the memory of your touch
and all the other little things
I've come to treasure so much.
You cannot go beyond my thoughts
or leave my love behind
because I keep you in my heart
and forever in my mind.

A mother's faith

It is a mother's faith
in our Father above
that fills the home
with happiness
and the heart
with truth and love!

What is a Mother?

It takes a mother's love
to make a house a home,
a place to be remembered
no matter where we roam.

It takes a mother's patience
to bring a child up right,
and her courage and her cheerfulness
to make a dark day bright.

It takes a mother's thoughtfulness
to mend the heart's deep hurts,
and her skill and her endurance
to mend little socks and shirts.

It takes a mother's kindness
to forgive us when we err,
to sympathize in trouble
and bow her head in prayer.

It takes a mother's wisdom
to recognize our needs
and to give us reassurance
by her loving words and deeds.

God, grant me …

Courage and hope for every day,
faith to guide me along my way,
understanding and wisdom, too,
and grace to accept
what life gives me to do.

People were also bringing babies to Jesus to have Him touch them. When the disciples saw this, they rebuked them. But Jesus called the children to Him and said, "Let the little children come to Me, and do not hinder them, for the kingdom of God belongs to such as these."

LUKE 18:15-16

For one who gives so much to others

It's not the things that can be bought
that are life's richest treasure,
it's just the little heart gifts
that money cannot measure.

A cheerful smile, a friendly word,
a sympathetic nod
are priceless little treasures
from the storehouse of our God.

There are things that can't be bought
with silver or with gold,
for thoughtfulness and kindness
and love are never sold.

They are the priceless things in life
for which no one can pay,
and the giver finds rich recompense
in giving them away.

And who on earth gives more away
and does more good for others
than understanding, kind and wise
and selfless, loving mothers ...

Who ask no more than just the joy
of helping those they love
to find in life the happiness
that they are dreaming of.

The LORD will guide you always;
He will satisfy your needs
in a sun-scorched land
and will strengthen your frame.
You will be like
a well-watered garden,
like a spring whose waters never fail.

ISAIAH 58:11

Showers of blessings

Each day there are showers of blessings
sent from the Father above,
for God is a great, lavish giver
and there is no end to His love -
His grace is more than sufficient,
His mercy is boundless and deep,
and His infinite blessings are countless
and all this we're given to keep,
if we but seek God and find Him
and ask for a bounteous measure
of this wholly immeasurable offering
from God's inexhaustible treasure -
For no matter how big man's dreams are,
God's blessings are infinitely more,
for always God's giving is greater
than what man is asking for.

Sow for yourselves righteousness,
reap the fruit of unfailing love,
and break up your unplowed
ground; for it is time to seek
the LORD, until He comes and
showers righteousness on you.

HOSEA 10:12

The art of greatness

It's not fortune or fame
or worldwide acclaim
that makes for true greatness,
you'll find –
It's the wonderful art
of teaching the heart
to always be
thoughtful and kind.

Teach me

Teach me to give of myself,
in whatever way I can,
of whatever I have to give.
Teach me to value myself,
my time, my talents,
my purpose, my life,
my meaning in Your world.

For we are God's workmanship,
created in Christ Jesus
to do good works,
which God prepared
in advance for us to do.

EPHESIANS 2:10

This is all I ask

Lord, show me the way
I can somehow repay
the blessings You've given me.

Lord, teach me to do
what You most want me to
and to be what You want me to be.

I'm unworthy I know
but I do love You so -
I beg You to answer my plea.

I've not got much to give
but as long as I live
may I give it completely to Thee!

An Easter promise

If we but had the eyes to see
God's face in every cloud,
if we but had the ears to hear
His voice above the crowd,
if we could feel His gentle touch
in every Springtime breeze
and find a haven in His arms
'neath sheltering, leafy trees.

If we could just lift up our hearts
like flowers to the sun
and trust His Easter Promise
and pray, "Thy will be done,"
we'd find the peace we're seeking,
the kind no man can give,
the peace that comes from knowing
He died so we might live!

"Peace I leave with you;
My peace I give you. I do not give
to you as the world gives.
Do not let your hearts be troubled
and do not be afraid."

JOHN 14:27

Love: God's gift divine

Love is enduring
and patient and kind,
it judges all things
with the heart not the mind,
and love can transform
the most commonplace
into beauty and splendor
and sweetness and grace.

For love is unselfish,
giving more than it takes,
and no matter what happens
love never forsakes.

It's faithful and trusting
and always believing,
guileless and honest
and never deceiving.

Yes, love is beyond
what man can define,
for love is immortal
and God's gift is divine!

May your *father*
and *mother*
be glad: may she who
gave
you birth *rejoice!*

PROVERBS 23:25

The true gift

With our hands we give gifts
that money can buy -
diamonds that sparkle
like stars in the sky,
trinkets that glitter
like the sun as it rises,
beautiful baubles
that come as surprises.
But only our hearts
can feel real love
and share the gift
of our Father above.

I love you

I love you for so many things,
I don't know where to start,
but most of all I love you
for your understanding heart –

A heart that makes you thoughtful
and considerate and kind,
a heavenly combination
that is difficult to find.

And I can't help the feeling
that loving folks like you
sent out so many prayer waves
that my dearest dream came true.

A priceless treasure

Love is like a priceless treasure
which there is no way to measure.
For who can fathom stars or sea
or figure the length of eternity?

Love's too great to understand,
but just to clasp a loved one's hand
can change the darkness into light
and make the heart take wingless flight,
and blessed are they who walk in love,
for love's a gift from God above.

*How great is the love the
Father has lavished on us, that we
should be called children of God!
And that is what we are!*

1 JOHN 3:1

The gift
of lasting love

Love is much more
than a tender caress
and more than
bright hours of gay happiness.

For a lasting love
is made up of sharing
both hours that are joyous
and also despairing.

It's made up of patience
and deep understanding
and never of stubborn
and selfish demanding.

It's made up of climbing
the steep hills together
and facing with courage
life's stormiest weather.

And nothing on earth
or in heaven can part
a love that has grown
to be part of the heart.

And just like the sun
and the stars and the sea,
this love will go on
through eternity.

For true love lives on
when earthly things die,
for it's part of the spirit
that soars to the sky.

Life will be brighter than noonday, and darkness will become like morning. You will be secure, because there is hope; you will look about you and take your rest in safety.

JOB 11:17-18

The joys of remembering

There's a heap of satisfaction
to sit here thinking of you
and to tell you once again, dear,
how very much I love you.

There is comfort just in longing
for a smile from your dear face,
and joy in just remembering
each sweet and fond embrace.

There is happiness in knowing
that my heart will always be
a place where I can hold you
and keep you near to me.

Blessings

My blessings are so many,
my troubles are so few,
how can I feel discouraged
when I know that I have You.

And I have the sweet assurance
that I'll never stand alone
if I but keep remembering
I am Yours and Yours alone.

So, in this world of trouble
with darkness all around,
take my hand and lead me
until I stand on higher ground.

For anything and everything
can somehow be endured
if Your presence is beside me
and lovingly assured !

*From the fullness
of His grace
we have all received
one blessing after another.*

JOHN 1:16

Open my eyes

God, open my eyes
so I may see
and feel Your presence
close to me ...

Give me strength
for my stumbling feet
as I battle the crowd
on life's busy street.

And widen the vision
of my unseeing eyes
so in passing faces I'll recognize
not just a stranger,
unloved and unknown,
but a friend with a heart
that is much like my own.

Give me perception
to make me aware
that scattered profusely
on life's thoroughfare
are the best gifts of God
that we daily pass by
as we look at the world
with unseeing eye.

A sure way to a happy day

Happiness is something
we create in our mind,
it's not something you search for
and so seldom find.

It's just waking up
and beginning the day
by counting our blessings
and kneeling to pray.

It's giving up thoughts
that breed discontent
and accepting what comes
as a gift heaven-sent.

It's giving up wishing
for things we have not
and making the best of
whatever we've got.

It's knowing that life
is determined for us,
and pursuing our tasks
without fret, fume, or fuss.

For it's by completing
what God gives us to do
that we find real contentment
and happiness too.

The joy of unselfish giving

Time is not measured
by the years that you live,
but by the deeds that you do
and the joy that you give.

And each day as it comes
brings a chance to each one
to love to the fullest,
leaving nothing undone
that would brighten the life
or lighten the load
of some weary traveler
lost on life's road.

So what does it matter
how long we may live
if as long as we live
we unselfishly give.

Climb till your
dreams come true

Often your tasks will be many,
and more than you think you can do.
Often the road will be rugged
and the hills insurmountable, too.

But always remember, the hills ahead
are never as steep as they seem,
and with faith in your heart start upward
and climb till you reach your dream.

For nothing in life that is worthy
is ever too hard to achieve
if you have the courage to try it
and you have the faith to believe.

For faith is a force that is greater
than knowledge or power or skill,
and many defeats turn to triumphs
if you trust in God's wisdom and will.

For faith is a mover of mountains,
there's nothing that God cannot do,
so start out today with faith in your heart
and climb till your dreams come true!

All things are possible with God!

Nothing is ever too hard to do
if your faith is strong
and your purpose is true ...
So never give up
and never stop
just journey on
to the mountaintop!

Priceless treasures

What could I give you
that would truly please
in topsy-turvy times like these?

I can't give you freedom from vexations,
or even lessen your irritations;
I can't take away or even make less
the things that annoy,
disturb, and distress;
For stores don't sell a single thing
to make the heart
that's troubled sing.

They sell the new look, suave and bland,
but nothing that lends a helping hand.

They sell rare gifts that are ultrasmart
but nothing to warm or comfort the heart.

The joys of life that cheer and bless,
the stores don't sell, I must confess.

But friends and prayers
are priceless treasures
beyond all monetary measures.

And so I say a special prayer
that God will keep you in His care.

And if I can ever help you, Mother dear,
in any way throughout the year,
you've only to call, for as long as I live
such as I have, I freely give!

Do not be anxious about anything,
but in everything,
by prayer and petition,
with thanksgiving,
present your requests to God.

*And the peace of God, which
transcends all understanding,
will guard your hearts
and your minds in Christ Jesus.*

PHILIPPIANS 4:6-7

Just because
you're you

May the knowledge
that your children
and their sweet children, too,
care for you and love you
just because you're you,
keep you ever happy
when lonely hours appear
in knowing that their love for you
is all around you, Mother dear.

*The boundary lines
have fallen for me
in pleasant places;
surely I have
a delightful inheritance.*

PSALM 16:6

Life's fairest flower

I have a garden within my soul
of wondrous beauty rare
wherein the blossoms of all my life
bloom ever in splendor fair.

The fragrance and charm of that garden,
where all of life's flowers bloom,
fill my aching heart with sweet content,
and banish failure's gloom.

Each flower a message is bringing,
a mem'ry of someone dear,
a picture of deepest devotion,
dispelling all doubt and fear.

Amid all this beauty and splendor,
one flower stands forth as queen -
Alone in her dazzling beauty,
alone but ever supreme.

This flower of love and devotion,
has guided me all through life,
strengthening my grief and my sorrow,
sharing my toil and my strife.

This flower has helped me to conquer
temptation so black and grim
and led me to victory and honor,
over my enemy - sin.

I have vainly sought in my garden,
through blossoms of love and light,
for a flower of equal wonder,
to compare with this one so bright.

But ever I've met with failure,
my search has been in vain -
For never a flower existed,
like the blossom I can claim.

For after years I now can see,
amid life's roses and rue,
God's greatest gift - to a little child,
my darling mother was you.

Whatever you do,
do it all for
the glory of God.

1 CORINTHIANS 10:31

The autumn of life

What a wonderful time is life's autumn
when the leaves
of the trees are all gold,
when God fills each day,
as He sends it,
with memories, priceless and old.

What a treasure house filled
with rare jewels
are the blessings of year upon year,
when life has been lived
as you've lived it
in a home
where God's presence is dear.

And may the deep meaning
surrounding this day,
like the paintbrush of God up above,
touch your life
with wonderful blessings
and fill your heart brimful with love!

Other books
in this range

ISBN: 1-86920-356-9

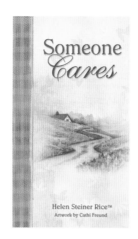

ISBN: 1-86920-358-5

ISBN: 1-86920-359-3